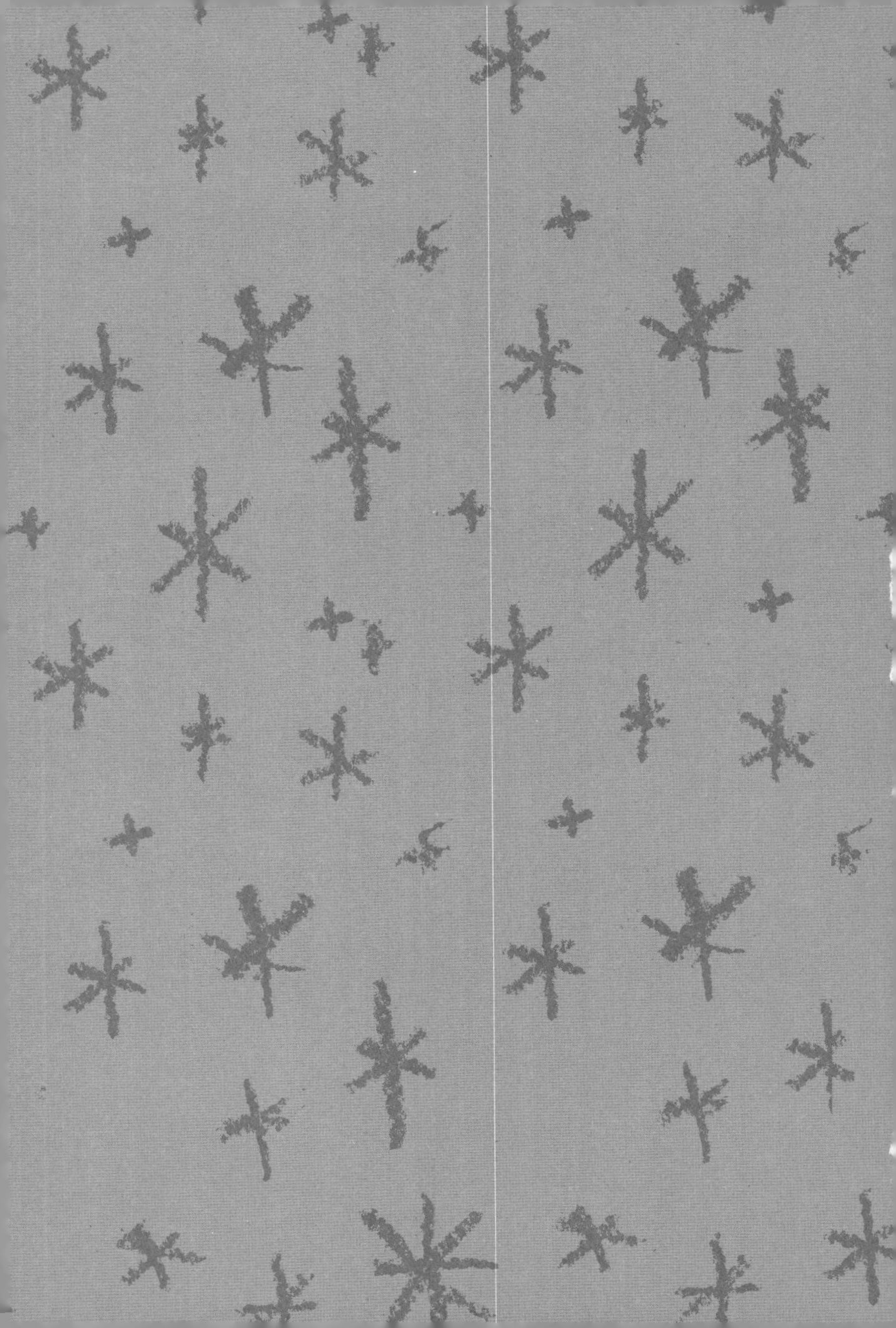

Monkeyfarts!

Library of Congress Cataloging in Publication Number: 2012934570
ISBN: 978-1-59474-605-5

Printed in China
Typeset in Burbank and Baskerville

Designed by Doogie Horner
Illustrations by Brian Biggs
Production management by John J. McGurk

Quirk Books
215 Church St.
Philadelphia, PA 19106
quirkbooks.com
10 9 8 7 6 5 4 3

Monkeyfarts!

Wacky Jokes Every Kid Should Know

By David Borgenicht

QUIRK BOOKS
PHILADELPHIA

This book is dedicated to my own two comedians, Sophie and Max. You make me laugh every day.

Introd

FOUR CAVEMEN are sitting around a fire, eating their latest kill.

One of them stands up, raises his food, and says, “Oooogah!” Everyone cracks up and continues eating. Another caveman stands up, raises his food, and says, “Ooooooooogah!” The group cracks up again. A third caveman stands, raises his food, and says, “Ooooogah oooogah!” Everyone rolls on the floor of the cave in laughter.

Not wanting to be left out, a fourth caveman stands and says, “Ooooogah oooogah oooogah!” There is complete silence—no laughter at all. Embarrassed, he sits back down.

After an uncomfortable silence, the third caveman turns to the fourth caveman, pats him on the back, and whispers, “Don’t worry about it. Some

uction

people can tell a joke, and some people can't."

Just then, the fourth caveman emits a huge fart that echoes throughout the cave.

Everyone rolls on the floor in laughter.

"I've still got it!" says the fourth caveman.

Welcome to *Monkeyfarts!* the ultimate unscientifically kid-tested and parent-approved joke book. Every joke in here has been read, told, and laughed at by kids (and a handful of adults). Every joke in here is guaranteed to make someone laugh.

Here's hoping that someone is you.

What's invisible and smells like bananas?
Monkeyfarts!

How are a firefly and an alien's farts alike?
They both glow in the dark.

What happened to the blind skunk?
He fell in love with a fart.

What's invisible, smelly, and hangs in a museum?
Fartwork.

Four Di-stink-tive (get it?) Bathroom Jokes

A BOY WAS AT A PUBLIC POOL and the lifeguard blew his whistle and yelled, "Hey, quit peeing in the pool!" The boy replied, "But everybody does it!" The lifeguard said, "Not from the diving board."

A LITTLE BOY WAS ABOUT TO sit on the toilet when an elf appeared in the toilet bowl.
"How long have you been in there?" asked the boy.
"Many moons," said the elf.

Why did Tigger stick his head in the toilet?
He was looking for Pooh.

What flies through the air, says "supercalifragilisticexpialidocious," and smells terrible?
Mary Poopins.

The Penguins and the Policeman

A POLICEMAN SEES A MAN walking down the street with four penguins. He says to the man, "Sir, are those your pet penguins?" "Yes," says the man. "Well, you should take those penguins to the zoo!" says the cop. "Good idea," says the man. And off they go. The next day the policeman sees the man again, and he's still with the penguins. But they are all wearing sunglasses. "Didn't I tell you to take those penguins to the zoo?" says the policeman. "Yes!" replies the man. "I did! And they liked it so much that today we're going to the beach!"

A MAN IS WATCHING TV when he hears a knock at the door. He opens the door and doesn't see anyone at first—then he looks down and sees a snail sitting there. He picks up the snail and throws it into the garden. Three months later, he's sitting and watching TV again when he hears another knock. He opens the door and sees the snail sitting there again. "Now what did you do that for?" asks the snail.

What did the snail say when he climbed onto the turtle's back?

"Wheeeeeeeeeeee!"

A TURTLE IS OUT FOR A WALK when he's mugged by four snails. After recovering his wits, he goes to make a police report. "Can you describe the snails?" asks the officer. "Not very well," replies the turtle. "It all happened so fast."

Why did the chicken cross the road?

To get to the other side.

Why did the chewing gum cross the road?

It was stuck to the chicken.

Why did the chicken cross the playground?

To get to the other slide.

What do you call a chicken at the North Pole?

Lost.

Is chicken soup good for you?

Not if you're a chicken.

Max and the Glass of Water

A FATHER HAS JUST PUT his son Max to bed. Five minutes later, Max calls out, "Da-ad . . ." His father goes into Max's room and asks, "What?" Max says, "I'm thirsty. Can you bring me a glass of water?" "No. It's time for lights-out," says the dad. Five minutes go by and Max calls out again. "Da-aaaad . . ." Getting frustrated, his father goes back into Max's room. "What?" "I'm thirsty! Can I have a glass of water?" "I told you no!" the father says. "If you ask again I'm going to have to spank you!" The father leaves the room. Five minutes later, Max calls out again. "Daaaa-aaaAAAAD . . ." "WHAT??!!" yells the father from downstairs. "When you come in to spank me, can you bring me a glass of water?"

Three "A Blank Walks into a Blank" Jokes

A horse walks into a diner, sits down, and says, "I'd like a bowl of apples, please." The waitress says, "OK, but why the long face?"

A man walks into a bar and says, "OW!"

A PIG WALKS INTO A RESTAURANT and orders ten sodas. He drinks them all, one right after the other. When he finishes the last one, the waiter says, "Don't you need to know where the bathroom is?" The pig says, "No, I go wee wee wee all the way home."

How do you know if there's an
elephant under your bed?
You bump your nose on the ceiling.

What do giraffes have
that no other animal has?
Baby giraffes.

What do you get when you cross a daffodil
with a crocodile?
I don't know, but whatever it is, don't sniff it.

What says "quick, quick"?
A duck with hiccups.

What did one flea say to the other flea
as they were heading out?
"Shall we walk or take the dog?"

How does a hammerhead shark
use a hammer?
He doesn't need one. He's a shark.

What's a dog's favorite job?

Rufferee.

The Kid and the Ice Cream Store

A KID RUNS INTO an ice cream store and asks for 24 scoops of ice cream. When the server has scooped all the ice cream, the kid wolfs it down as fast as he can. The server says, "Wow, I've never seen anyone eat that fast before!" The kid says, "You'd eat that fast too if you had what I have." The server says, "What do you have?" The kid says, "Only 25 cents," and runs out of the store.

Q	A
What did Tarzan say when he heard the elephants coming?	“Here come the elephants!”
Why do elephants never forget?	Because nobody ever tells them anything.
What's brown and sticky?	A stick.
Why was the chicken afraid of the chicken?	It was chicken.

WHAT'S IN THE MIDDLE OF A JELLYFISH?

A JELLYBUTTON.

•

WHAT DO DUCKS WATCH ON TV?

DUCKUMENTARIES.

•

WHAT DO YOU GET WHEN YOU CROSS A DOG WITH AN ELEPHANT?

A VERY NERVOUS MAILMAN.

The Duck and the Grocery Store

A DUCK WALKS INTO a grocery store and asks, “Got any duck food?” The clerk says, “No, we don’t carry duck food.” So the duck waddles away. The next day the duck comes back and asks, “Got any duck food?” The clerk says, “You came in yesterday—I told you we don’t carry duck food.” So the duck waddles away. The next day the duck comes back in. “Got any duck food?” “No!” says the clerk. “And if you come back in here one more time to ask for duck food, I’m going to nail your bill to the counter!” The next day, the duck comes back in. “Got any nails?” asks the duck. “No, we don’t,” says the clerk. “Well, then, have you got any duck food?”

What did Godzilla say to King Kong when he was on top of the Empire State Building?

"Watch out for that first step. It's a doozy."

What did Godzilla have at the all-you-can-eat restaurant?

The waiters.

WHAT DO YOU FIND BETWEEN GODZILLA'S TOES?

SLOW RUNNERS.

Why does Darth Vader like his toast to be burnt on one side?
Because he prefers the dark side.

Knock, knock.
Who's there?
Interrupting wookie.
Interrupting wookie–
MWAAAAAAAAAGGGH!

Why did they call it the Death Star?
What are they supposed to call it, the Bahamas?

What's blue and white and goes "Beep-boop ow! Beep-boop ow! Beep-boop ow!"?
R2D2 falling down the stairs.

How does Luke get into the Imperial Base?
Ewoks.

The Mystery of the Talking Cheese

A KID GOES TO THE GROCERY store with his dad. He stops at a table with a tray full of little samples of cheese and hears a voice say, "You've got nice hair." The kid looks all around but can't see where the voice is coming from. He takes a sample of the cheese and hears the same voice say, "You are a very smart boy!" The boy is confused by this, so he asks a grocery clerk what is going on. "I think this store is haunted," says the boy. The clerk just laughs and says, "No, it's the cheese. Didn't you read the sign? It's complimentary."

What's a prehistoric monster
called when it sleeps?
A dinosnore.

Knock, knock.
Who's there?
Ivana.
Ivana who?
Ivana drink your blood!

Why don't monsters eat clowns?
Because they taste funny.

Why is it safe to tell a mummy your secret?
Because he'll keep it under wraps.

Do monsters eat popcorn
with their fingers?
No, they eat the fingers separately.

How many vampires does it take to screw in a lightbulb?
None. They like it in the dark.

The Frog and the Psychic

A FROG GOES TO SEE a psychic. The psychic tells him, “You will meet a beautiful young girl who will want to know everything about you.” The frog is excited. “This is great! Will I meet her in the forest, by a wishing well?” the frog asks. “No,” says the psychic, “in her biology class, on the dissection table.”

What did the polar bear say when it saw tourists in sleeping bags?
"Mmmm, burritos."

Why are igloos round?
So polar bears can't hide in the corners.

How does a polar bear stop a DVD?
He presses the paws button.

Four Wonderful "What's Yellow" Jokes

What's yellow and goes clickity-click?
A ballpoint banana.

•

What's yellow on the inside and green on the outside?
A banana dressed up as a cucumber.

•

What's big, yellow, and can kill you if it falls out of a tree?
A bulldozer.

What's yellow and dangerous?

A canary with a machine gun.

The Boy and the Math Teacher

A MATH TEACHER asked a little boy, "If you had one dollar and you asked your father for five more, how many would you have?"

"One dollar," replied the boy.

"No. You'd have six dollars!" said the teacher. "You obviously don't know your addition."

"And you obviously don't know my father," said the boy.

Why did the detective bring a blanket to the stakeout?

Because the captain told him he was going undercover.

Why did the robber take a shower?

He wanted to make a clean getaway.

What do you call a duck that wears a mask and steals things?

A robber duckie.

Four Whip-Smart "What" Jokes

What has wheels and flies?
A garbage truck.

What did the nut say when it sneezed?
Cashew!

What pet does everyone have?
An armpet.

What room has no walls?
A mushroom.

The Man and the Cross-Eyed Dog

A MAN TAKES HIS DOG to the vet. "My dog's cross-eyed. He's always running into things, and I don't think he can see very well. Is there anything you can do for him?"

"Well," says the vet, "let's have a look at him." So the vet picks up the dog. He examines his eyes, ears, and teeth. He takes his temperature. He feels his stomach.

Finally, he says, "I'm going to have to put this dog down."

"What!" says the man, very upset. "Just because he's cross-eyed?"

"No," says the vet. "Because he's really heavy."

Four Fabulous Bird Jokes

Why do seagulls fly over the sea?
Because if they flew over the bay they would be baygulls.

What kind of crows stick together?
Vel-crows.

Why do ducks have webbed feet?
To put out forest fires.

WHY DO FLAMINGOS STAND ON ONE LEG?
BECAUSE IF THEY PULLED UP THE OTHER LEG, THEY'D FALL DOWN.

The Books and the Chickens

A COUPLE OF CHICKENS walk up to the checkout desk at a public library and say, "Buk Buk BUK." The librarian decides that the chickens want three books. She gets three books that she thinks they will like and checks them out to them. The chickens take the books and leave.

Around lunchtime, the chickens return to the desk. They seem upset and say, "Buk Buk BuKKOOK!" The librarian figures the chickens want three more books, so she finds three more suitable chicken books for them. The chickens take them and leave.

Later that afternoon, the chickens come back to the library. They find the librarian—they are looking

very upset. They say, "Buk Buk Buk Buk Bukkooook!" The librarian is now suspicious of these chickens. She gives them five more books, but decides to follow them when they leave the library.

She follows them out of the library and down the street to a park. She hides behind a tree and watches. The chickens throw the books at a frog in a pond, and the frog says, "Rrredit Rrredit Rrredit . . ."

The Telemarketer and the Little Boy

A TELEMARKETER CALLS a house, and a little boy answers in a whisper.

"Hello?"

The salesperson says, "Can I speak to your mommy?"

"She's busy," whispers the boy.

"What about your daddy?"

"He's busy too," the boy whispers.

"Is there anyone else in the house?" asks the telemarketer.

"Yes," says the boy. "A policewoman and a fireman."

"A policewoman and a fireman! Can I speak to one of them?"

"No," whispers the boy. "They're busy too."

The telemarketer says, "Little boy, with all those adults in the house, what are they so busy doing?"

After a short pause, the little boy whispers, "They're looking for me."

What do you tell the teacher when she says you've missed a lot of school?

"Well, I didn't miss it too much!"

What do gnomes do after school?

Their gnomework.

Why did the clock get called into the principal's office?

It was tocking too much.

1

Knock, knock.
Who's there?
Amos.
Amos who?
A mosquito bit me!

2

Knock, knock.
Who's there?
Andy.
Andy who?
Andy bit me again!

3

Knock, knock.
Who's there?
Little old lady.
Little old lady who?
I didn't know you could yodel!

Knock, knock.
Who's there?
Cargo.
Cargo who?
Car go beep beep!

5

Knock, knock.
Who's there?
Banana.
Banana who?
Knock, knock.
Who's there?
Banana.
Banana who?
Knock, knock.
Who's there?
Banana.
Banana who?
Knock knock.
Who's there?
Orange.
Orange who?
Orange you glad I didn't say banana again?

6

Knock, knock.
Who's there?
Obi Wan.
Obi Wan who?
Obi Wanna come in and teach you to be a Jedi.

7

Knock, knock.
Who's there?
Ima.
Ima who?
Ima gonna break down the door if you don't let me in!

8

Knock, knock.
Who's there?
Toby.
Toby who?
Toby or not toby, that is the question!

Knock, knock.
Who's there?
Harriet.
Harriet who?
Harry ate my dinner, do you have any more?

10

Will you remember me tomorrow? (Yes)
Will you remember me in a week? (Yes)
Will you remember me in a year? (Yes)
Knock, knock.
Who's there?
Don't you remember me?

The Traveling Salesman

A TRAVELING SALESMAN walks into a hotel and asks for a room.

"We are all full," says the desk clerk.

"But all the other hotels are full, too," says the salesman. "Are you sure you don't have one room?"

"I already told you. We're full up, and no rooms are available."

The salesman thinks for a moment, and says, "If I were the president of the United States, would you have a room for me?"

"Sure," says the clerk. "If you were the president, I would."

"Well then," says the salesman, "I'll take his room, because he's not coming."

Why did Little Miss Muffet sit on her tuffet?
Because "chair" doesn't rhyme with "Muffet."

Why did the bird join the Air Force?
He wanted to be a parrot trooper.

Why don't you see giraffes in elementary school?
Because they're all in high school.

Why can't you tell jokes to an egg?
Because it will crack up.

Four Jolly Jungle Jokes

Q	A
Why shouldn't you play cards in the jungle?	Because of all the cheetahs!
Why do gorillas have big nostrils?	Because they have big fingers.
What's black and white and red all over?	A zebra with a sunburn.
What do you call memory loss in a parrot?	Polynesia.

The Little Old Lady and the Dog

A MAN IS WALKING through the park when he sees a little old lady and a dog sitting on a bench.

He walks up to the lady and asks, “Ma’am, does your dog bite?”

“No,” says the lady.

He goes to pet the dog, and it angrily nips his hand.

“I thought you said your dog didn’t bite!” says the man.

“He doesn’t,” says the lady. “But that’s not my dog.”

What's the difference between Prince Charles, a bald man, and a monkey's mother?
One is the heir apparent, one has no hair apparent, and one is a hairy parent!

What do you get when you cross a balloon with a porcupine?

POP!

Why are elephants so wrinkly?
Have you ever tried to iron one?

•

What time is it when an elephant sits on your fence?
Time to get a new fence!

•

What game do elephants like to play most?
Squash.

•

How can you tell if there's been an elephant in the fridge?
There are footprints in the butter.

•

What do you give an elephant that's about to puke?
Plenty of space.

The Little Girl and the Doctor

A LITTLE GIRL GOES TO see the doctor. She's got a pea in one nostril, a grape in the other, and a string bean stuck in her ear.

She says to the doctor, "I don't feel good."

The doctor replies, "Well, you're obviously not eating right!"

WHAT DO YOU CALL A FISH WITHOUT AN EYE?

A FSH.

WHAT DID THE FISH SAY WHEN IT HIT A CONCRETE WALL?

DAM.

WHAT DO WHALES LIKE TO CHEW?

BLUBBER GUM.

Four Semi-Educational Jokes

What do Alexander the Great and Kermit the Frog have in common?
The same middle name.

Where was the Declaration of Independence signed?
At the bottom.

How did the Vikings send secret messages?
With Norse code.

What is an atom?
The guy who went out with Eve.

What's green and purple and goes up and down?

Barney in an elevator.

What's small and cuddly and bright purple?

A puppy holding its breath.

What do a grape and an elephant have in common?

They're both purple—except for the elephant.

What's a cat's favorite color?

Purr-ple.

What does the green grape say to the purple grape?

He screams, "Breathe, breathe!"

Two Strings at the Diner

THERE ARE THESE TWO strings walking down the road when they come to a diner. They decide to stop in and have a bite to eat. So they sit down at a table and notice that no one is coming to take their order. The first string decides to go to the counter. He asks the waiter if he can order some food. "Sorry," says the waiter, "but we don't serve strings here." So the first string returns to the table and tells the second string the problem. "It's okay," says the second string. "I'll take care of this." So the second string stands up, unravels his ends a bit, and ties himself into a knot. Then he walks up to the counter and asks to order. The waiter says, "I already told your friend, we don't serve strings. Aren't you a string?" "No," says the second string, "I'm a frayed knot."

What do you call a bearded man
who sits on his porch making pots?
A Hairy Potter.

What do you call James Bond when he takes a bath?

Bubble 07.

What do you call an
800-pound angry gorilla?
Whatever he wants you to call him.

What do you call an 800-pound angry gorilla wearing earmuffs?
Anything you like.
He can't hear you!

What do you call Batman and Robin if they get smashed by a steamroller?

Flatman and Ribbon.

•

Why does Superman's shirt fit so tight?

He's wearing a size S.

•

Where is Spider Man's home page?

On the World Wide Web.

Superman and Batman got into an argument and decided to get revenge on each other. Superman writes on the wall of the Batcave: "Batman is a sissy."
The next day Batman writes on the wall of the *Daily Planet*: "Superman is Clark Kent."

1

Knock, knock!
Who's there?
You know!
You know who?
It's okay, he's dead. You can say his name now.

2

What did Harry Potter say when he couldn't open the door to the Chamber of Secrets?
Dumb old door.

3

How do you know you're taking Harry Potter too seriously?
When your computer says you've got mail, you run outside looking for owls.

4

What does a Death Eater eat for breakfast?
A bowl of crucios.

WHAT COLOR ARE BURPS?

BURPLE.

•

WHY DID THE SKELETON BURP?

HE DIDN'T HAVE THE GUTS TO FART.

The Cowboy and the Lost Horse

A COWBOY RIDES INTO TOWN, goes into the saloon for a drink, walks outside, and finds his horse has been stolen. He walks into the saloon and fires his gun through the ceiling. "Which one of you stole my hoss?" he yells. No one answers. "All right, I'm gonna have another drink, and if my hoss ain't outside by the time I finish, I'm gonna do what I done in Texas!" He has another drink, walks outside, and his horse is back where it was. So he gets on it, ready to ride out of town. The bartender wanders out of the saloon and says, "Glad you got your hoss back, partner. So what did happen in Texas?" The cowboy turns to him and says, "I had to walk all the way home."

When does a pirate say, "Shiver me timbers"?

When his wooden leg is in the freezer.

What's a pirate's favorite letter? RRRRRRRR.	What's a pirate's second favorite letter? C.
How much does it cost for a pirate to pierce his ears? A buck an ear.	Why do pirates go on vacation? To get a little arrrrrr and arrrrrr.

Five Hardy Har Har "How Do You" Jokes

How do you make a bandstand?
Hide all their chairs.

HOW DO YOU CATCH A UNIQUE RABBIT?
UNIQUE UP ON IT.

HOW DO YOU CATCH A TAME RABBIT?
TAME WAY, UNIQUE UP ON IT.

How do you fit four elephants in a Mini Cooper?
Two in the front and two in the back.

How do you make a tissue dance?
Put a little boogie in it.

The Polar Bear in the Ice Cream Store

A POLAR BEAR WALKS into an ice cream store and says to the clerk, "I'll have a hot fudge . . . sundae."

"Okay," says the clerk. "But why the big pause?"

The polar bear looks down at his hands and says, "What do you mean? I've always had them."

What's smaller than
an ant's mouth?
An ant's dinner.

Why don't anteaters
ever get sick?
They're full of anty bodies.

How many ants does it
take to fill an apartment?
Tenants.

What did the Pink Panther say
when he stepped on an ant?
Dead ant, dead ant . . . dead
ant, dead ant, dead ant.

HOW DOES AN ANT THANK HIS FRIENDS FOR HELPING HIM BUILD AN ANTHILL?

THANK YOU THANK YOU
THANK YOU THANK YOU
THANK YOU THANK YOU
THANK YOU THANK YOU
THANK YOU THANK YOU
THANK YOU THANK YOU
THANK YOU THANK YOU
THANK YOU THANK YOU
THANK YOU THANK YOU
THANK YOU THANK YOU
THANK YOU THANK YOU
THANK YOU THANK YOU

THANK YOU THANK YOU
THANK YOU THANK YOU
THANK YOU THANK YOU
THANK YOU THANK YOU
THANK YOU THANK YOU
THANK YOU THANK YOU
THANK YOU THANK YOU
THANK YOU THANK YOU
THANK YOU THANK YOU
THANK YOU THANK YOU
THANK YOU THANK YOU
THANK YOU THANK YOU
THANK YOU THANK YOU
THANK YOU THANK YOU
THANK YOU THANK YOU
THANK YOU THANK YOU
THANK YOU THANK YOU . . .

Harpo the Cat

JOE AND DAVE WERE BROTHERS who lived with their elderly mother and Dave's pet cat Harpo. Dave went away on business and asked his brother Joe to look after Harpo. On the first night away, Dave called Joe and asked him how Harpo was doing.

"Harpo is dead," said Joe.

Dave was shocked. "That's a terrible way to deliver bad news!"

"How should I have told you?" asked Joe.

"You should have broken it to me gently," said Dave. "You could have said that Harpo got up onto the roof of the house, and that you had to call the fire department to get him down. You could have said that Harpo tried to jump, and that they had to rush him to the hospital, where eventually, after a long battle, he died."

"Sorry about that," said Joe.

"It's okay," said Dave. "By the way, how's Mom doing?"

Joe pauses and then says, "Well, she got up onto the roof . . . "

Four Somewhat Obvious "What" Jokes

What did the hat say to the scarf?

You hang around while I go on a head.

What two things can't you have for breakfast?

Lunch and dinner.

What does a tree do when it's ready to go home?

It leaves.

What do you call two people who embarrass you in front of your friends?

Mom and Dad.

Good News and Bad News

A DOCTOR WALKS INTO the recovery room to talk to a patient he has just operated on.

"I have good news and bad news," he tells the patient.

"What's the bad news?" asks the patient.

"The bad news is that we've looked at your X-rays, and you have to go back into surgery."

"Ugh," says the patient. "What's the good news?"

"I found the scalpel we were missing!"

Two Big Bird Jokes

WHAT DO YOU CALL A SICK EAGLE?

ILL EAGLE.

WHAT'S ORANGE AND SOUNDS LIKE A PARROT?

A CARROT.

Two Lovely Lobster Jokes

Where does a lobster keep his clothes?
In the clawset.

Why can't lobsters share?
Because they are shellfish.

The Missing Cookies

A GIRL WALKS INTO the kitchen first thing in the morning to find her mother holding a cookie jar and tapping her foot angrily.

"Young lady," says her mom, "last night I left two cookies in the jar, and now there's only one. How do you explain that?"

"I guess it was so dark I missed the second one," says the girl.

Why did Snow White eat the poisoned apple?
She was hungry.

Why wasn't Cinderella any good at soccer?
She kept running away from the ball, and she only had one shoe.

What did Little Red Riding Hood say when she saw the big bad wolf?
Nothing. She didn't recognize him.

What kind of animal goes "OOM"?
A cow walking backwards!

What kind of shoes do frogs wear?
Open toad shoes.

Where do hamsters come from?

Hamsterdam.

The Vampire Bat

A VAMPIRE BAT FLIES BACK to his cave with blood on his mouth. The other bats stare at him and ask where he got the blood. He says, "Did you see that tree back there?"

"Sure," they reply.

"Well, I didn't!"

Q	A
What did the banana say to the gorilla?	Nothing–bananas can't talk.
What's a banana's favorite symphony?	Beethoven's Fifth ("Ba-na-na-naaaaa! Ba-na-na-naaaa!")
What is long and yellow and always points north?	A magnetic banana.
What do you do with a blue banana?	Try to cheer it up.

Which months have 28 days?

All of them.

Why was 6 afraid of 7?

Because 7 8 9!

What did Tiny Tim's mother call him when he turned 21?

Tim.

Who invented fractions?

Henry the Eighth.

What did the 0 say to the 8?

"Nice belt!"

The Boy, the Man, and the Doorbell

A MAN IS WALKING DOWN the street one day when he notices a very small boy trying to press a doorbell on a house.

But the boy is very small and the doorbell is too high for him to reach.

After watching the boy's efforts for a little while, the man comes over.

He walks up behind the little fellow and says, "Here, let me help you," and presses the doorbell.

Then, crouching down to the child's level, the man smiles kindly and asks, "And now what, my little man?"

The boy replies, "Now we run!"

WHAT DID THE COWBOY SAY WHEN HIS DOG LEFT?

DOGGONE!

•

HOW DO YOU STOP A CHARGING BULL?

YOU TAKE AWAY HIS CREDIT CARD.

Four "What, When, Where, and Why" Jokes

What starts with "T," ends with "T," and is full of "T"?

A teapot.

When is a door not a door?

When it's ajar.

Where does a general keep his armies?

In his sleevies.

Why did Captain Hook cross the road?

To get to the secondhand shop.

Talking Dog for Sale

A MAN SEES A SIGN that reads, "Talking Dog for Sale" and has to check it out.

"Do you really have a talking dog?" he asks the owner. The owner, looking frustrated, says, "Come on in. I'd love to get rid of him."

The guy goes in and sees a normal looking black mutt. "So do you really talk?" asks the man. "Yep," the mutt replies. "Well, what's your story?"

The dog says, "I discovered I could talk when I was pretty young. I wanted to help the government, so I told the CIA. They had me flying from country to country, sitting in rooms with world leaders, because no one figured a dog would be eavesdropping. I was one of their most valuable spies! I was awarded a bunch of medals, too. All that travel wore me out, though, so now I'm just retired."

The guy is amazed. He asks the owner what he wants for the dog. The owner says, "Ten dollars." The guy says, "This dog is amazing! Why on earth are you selling him so cheap?" The owner replies, "He's just a big liar. He didn't do any of that stuff."

What kind of security systems do fast-food joints have?
Burger alarms.

WHAT DID ONE SNOWMAN SAY TO THE OTHER SNOWMAN?
DO YOU SMELL CARROTS?

What do you call cheese that doesn't belong to you?
Nacho cheese.

What do you call a boomerang that doesn't work?
A stick.

What do you call a crate full of ducks?
A box of quackers.

WHAT HAPPENS WHEN A DUCK FLIES UPSIDE DOWN?
IT QUACKS UP.

Why do ducks watch the news?
For the feather forecast.

What does a duck get after he eats?
A bill.

The Hot Dogs in the Pot

TWO HOT DOGS were in a pot of water that got put on the stovetop. Soon the water started heating up. It started getting hotter and hotter. Pretty soon the water was almost boiling. "This water is almost boiling!" yelled one hot dog. "Oh my gosh," yelled the other one. "A talking hot dog!"

Three Moderately Gross Bathroom Jokes

What's a kid's favorite book to read in the bathroom after eating prunes?

Diarrhea of a Wimpy Kid.

•

Who do you call when you need help going poop?

The butler.

•

Why did the idiot decide to sleep in the toilet?

Because his friend told him he looked pooped!

1 **How do you hunt for bees?**

With bee bee guns.

What goes "99-clonk, 99-clonk, 99-clonk?" 2

A centipede with a wooden leg.

3 **What did one firefly say to the other?**

"I got to glow now."

What is the last thing to go through a bug's mind when he hits your windshield? 4

His butt.

Acknowledgments

Many thanks to the kids and parents who read this book in progress and contributed to the selection and fixing of it: The entire PR-D class at the Philadelphia School, Gene, Sam, Leo, Christine, Fergus and Eamonn, Rachel and Emily, Janet, Laurie, Kim, and, of course, Sophie and Max.

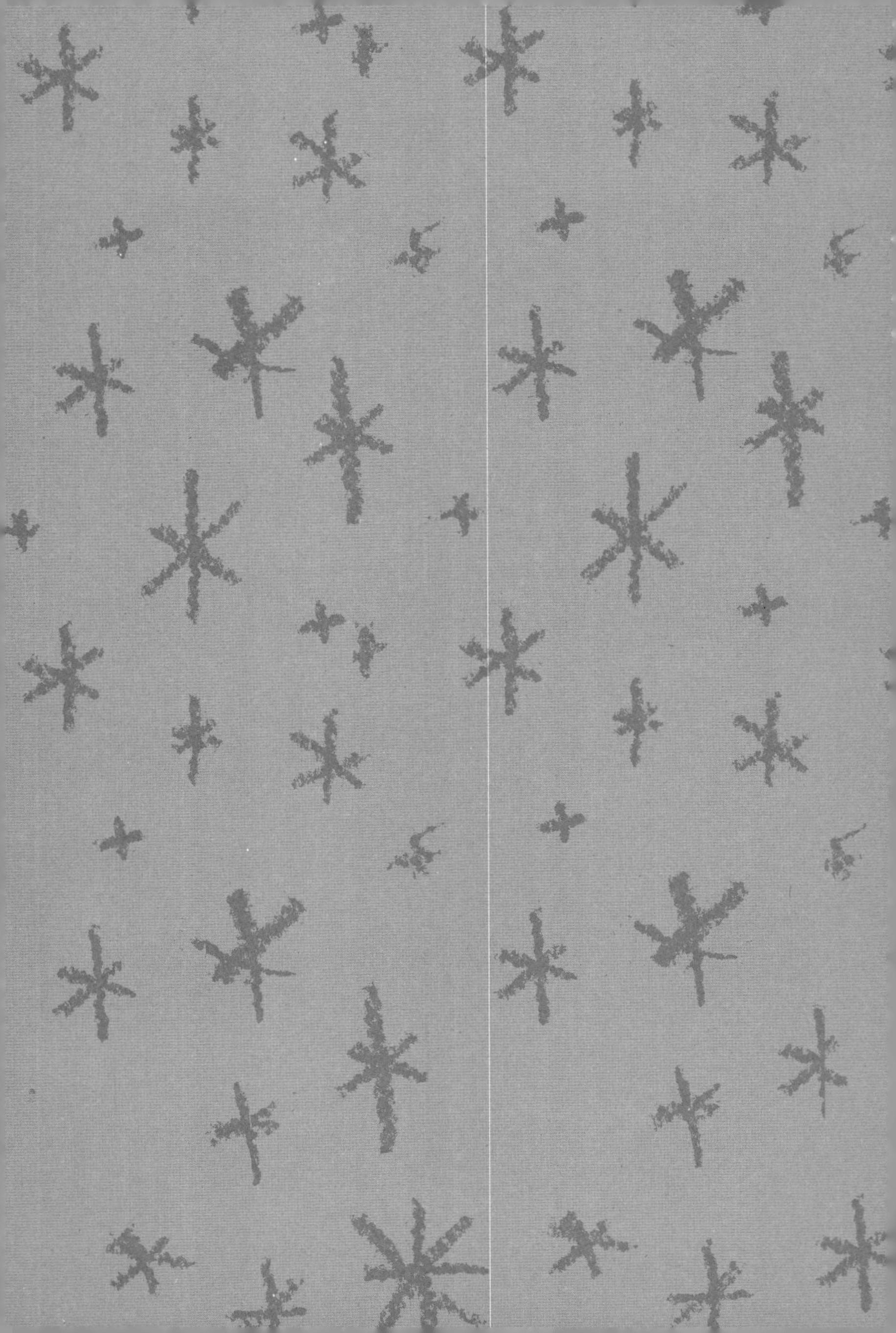